TRAIN

RISE UP

BASIC
TRAINING
FOR WARRIORS

NexGen® is an imprint of
Cook Communications Ministries, Colorado Springs, CO 80918
Cook Communications, Paris, Ontario
Kingsway Communications, Eastbourne, England

Rise Up: Training Manual
© Copyright 2006 by Ron Luce
Ron Luce is the founder and president of Teen Mania Ministries.

First printing 2006
Printed in Canada
    1 2 3 4 5 6 7 8 9 10   Printing/Year   11 10 09 08 07 06

Cover Design: Brand navigation, LLC
Interior Design: Helen Harrison

Full source citations can be found in the Rise Up: Basic Training for Warriors Leader's
Guide.

ISBN: 0-78144-319-9

NORMANDY, FRANCE JUNE 6, 1944.

THE NAZIS had stormed across Europe, pillaging and destroying the people and the land. They were determined to impose their ideology and values on the world, and they had conquered virtually every nation they desired. Even as they threatened England with total domination, **THEY SEEMED INDESTRUCTIBLE.** Yet plans were being laid for a strategic counterattack.

This counterattack is known as D-Day. **IT WAS DANGEROUS, RISKY, AND WELL-PLANNED.** And in the end, it turned the entire tide of World War II, paving the way for the Allies to defeat the Nazis.

TODAY WE FACE OUR OWN D-DAY. Our evil enemy marches across the land, leaving the ravished hearts and minds of teens in their wake. We can stand by and watch, or **WE CAN TAKE TO THE BATTLEFIELD AND BECOME WARRIORS.** This is a war for the heart and soul of this generation that **WE CAN WIN** if we all rise up and take action.

SO WHAT AM I GOING TO BE? A WATCHER OR A WARRIOR?

NUMB

ALLOWING YOURSELF TO BE HONEST

will help you bring to light the things that have held you back from pursuing God **WITH ALL YOUR HEART.**

Do I despise anyone?	YES	NO
Am I a jealous person?	YES	NO
Do I lie?	YES	NO
Do I put anything or anyone before God?	YES	NO
Do I swear?	YES	NO
Do I honor my parents?	YES	NO
Do I honor God with my body?	YES	NO
Am I greedy?	YES	NO
Am I a complainer?	YES	NO
Am I bitter?	YES	NO
Do I tell dirty jokes?	YES	NO
Do I get drunk?	YES	NO
Do I indulge in impure thoughts?	YES	NO

WHAT ELSE?

Dear God,

Sincerely,
Me

RISE UP!

○○○			New Message			○

| Send | Chat | Attach | Address | Fonts | Colors | Save As Draft |

To:

Cc:

Subject: Me and the lies I've been told

≡▾ **Account:** ⬍ **Signature:** None ⬍

WHAT ARE YOU WORTH?

The only one to run to (Deut. 33:27)
The apple of God's eye (Ps. 17:6–8)
He is good (Ps. 100:5)
Unfailing love will be a comfort to you (Ps. 119:76)
His banner over you is love (Song of Songs 2:4)
Unfailing love will never be shaken (Is. 54:10)
New mercies every day (Lam. 3:22–24)
Died before you knew (Rom. 5:8)
Unfathomable (1 Cor. 2:9)
Lavishes love on His child (1 John 3:1)
God is greater than our hearts (1 John 3:19–20)

JUST THREE WORDS

WHAT DOES HE SAY ABOUT ME?

You were created in His _____
(Gen. 1:27)

You are one of His _____
(Rom. 9:26)

You are His _____
(Jas. 1:18)

You can do _____ through Christ
(Phil. 4:13)

You are full of _____, _____, _____
(1 Cor. 1:30)

You are fearfully and _____ made
(Ps. 139:14)

UNDO THE LIES

THE LIES	THE TRUTH

We are spiritual beings having a human experience.
Pierre Teilhard De Chardin

SAYING NO IS TOUGH.

PRAY   What am I going to pray for?

CHOOSE   What choices am I going to make?

TALK   Who am I going to talk to?

KNOW   What does the Bible say?

CHANGE   How will I change? (be specific)

RISE UP!

U.S. children and teens average 38.5 hours a week watching TV, movies, videos, and playing computer and video games. (*Sex, Lies, and the Media*)

TV presents an average of eight "sexual incidents" during the 8 p.m. "family hour." (*USA Today*)

American kids spend more time watching TV than they spend in the classroom. (University of Missouri, Kansas City)

70% of 15-17 year olds say they stumble across pornography online very or somewhat often, and a majority of those exposed to it say they were "not too" or "not at all" upset by it. (Sharon Secor)

When asked to choose their favorite television commercial in a spring 2002 study, more teens named commercials for Budweiser than for any other brand including Pepsi, Nike, and Levi's. (Teenage Research Unlimited)

Over three-fourths (78%) of teens have been able to purchase Mature-rated video games. (Lion and the Lamb Project)

I will . . .

_____

_____

_____

_____

Sign here

X _____

THE SCRIPTURE:

THE PLAN OF ACTION:

MORE SCRIPTURES:

FRIENDS AND ACQUAINTANCES

Can you think of one friendship you have right now where you have never talked about God?

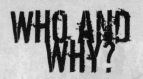

WHO AND WHY?

Do you need to go to someone and ask for their forgiveness or even offer your forgiveness?

WHO AND FOR WHAT?

You need to find a friend who will challenge you to stand strong in your walk with God and commit to an accountability relationship with them.

Who would make a good accountability partner?

_____

phone number: _____

email: _____

Can you think of a Christian adult who could support you as you walk through the real-life battlefield?

_____   could pray for me and support
          name   me with godly wisdom.

phone number:_____

e-mail:_____

MY FAMILY

How am I going to act differently around my family when I get home?

_____

_____

Do the thing you fear
and death of fear is certain.
Ralph W. Emerson

ALMOST ONE MILLION TEENAGE GIRLS GET PREGNANT each year.
(The Alan Guttmacher Institute)

Each year, approximately three million cases of **SEXUALLY TRANSMITTED DISEASES** occur among teenagers. This means one in every four sexually experienced teens contract an STD.
(The Alan Guttmacher Institute)

88% OF TEENAGERS who pledged to **REMAIN VIRGINS** until they are married ended up **HAVING SEX BEFORE MARRIAGE**.
(BBC News)

67% of sexually experienced teens wish they had **WAITED LONGER** to become sexually active.
(National Campaign to Prevent Teen Pregnancy)

ABOUT HALF of high school seniors are sexually active.
(Barna Research Online)

Is there someone that you have an unhealthy connection with? Is there a person in your life that you have an un-godly soul tie with? Is it possible that you have given someone a piece of your soul and didn't realize it until now?

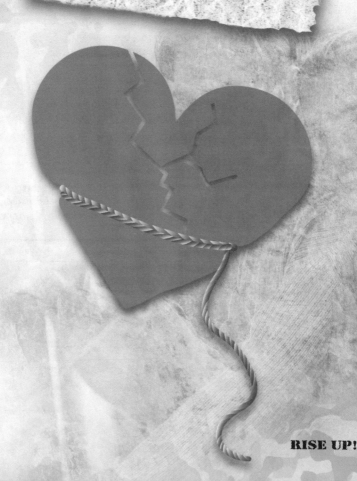

$$1 \times 1 = 1$$

$$1/2 \times 1 = 1/2$$

$$1/2 \times 1/2 = 1/4$$

How could these equations affect you now and in the future?

_____

_____

_____

_____

_____

_____

_____

_____

WHAT DO I NEED TO GET RID OF?

WHAT ARE YOU WIPING OUT OF YOUR LIFE TODAY?

WILL YOU CRUSH THE CRUSH?

Let your religion be less of a theory and more of a love affair.

GK Chesterton

50% OF HIGH SCHOOLERS report abusing alcohol. Alcohol kills 6.5 times more teenagers than all other illicit drugs combined. (FamilyFirstAid Help for Troubled Teens)

In 2003, **52.8%** of high school seniors reported **USING ILLICIT DRUGS** (marijuana, cocaine, heroin, hallucinogens, and others). (TeenDrugAbuse.us)

17% of high school students say they **HAVE CARRIED A GUN,** knife, or club to school in the past 30 days. (FamilyFirstAid Help for Troubled Teens)

DRIVING AFTER DRINKING killed 16,694 people in the year 2004. (NHTSA's National Center for Statistics and Analysis)

AS MANY AS 40% of kids have experimented with self-injury. (www.elizabethmore.com)

SUICIDE IS THE THIRD leading cause of **DEATH** among teenagers – **OVER 1,500 TEENS** kill themselves each year. (FamilyFirstAid Help for Troubled Teens)

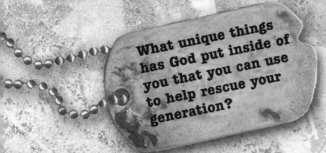

What unique things has God put inside of you that you can use to help rescue your generation?

RISE UP!

_____   _____

_____   _____

_____   _____

_____   _____

_____   _____

_____   _____

_____   _____

_____   _____

_____   _____

_____   _____

_____   _____

_____   _____

_____   _____

Give up your small ambitions.
J. Hudson Taylor

WILL YOU GO?

_____

_____

_____

_____

_____

_____

_____

_____

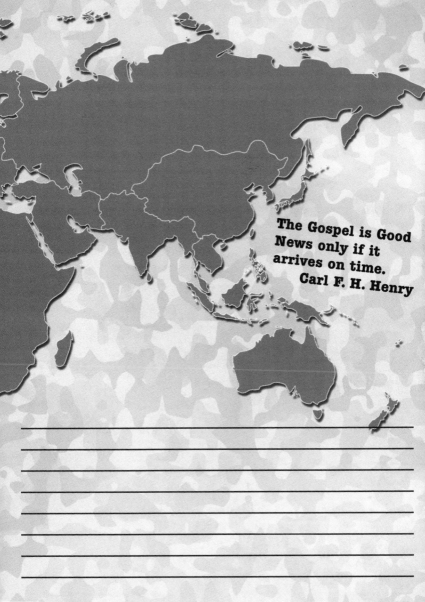

The Gospel is Good
News only if it
arrives on time.
Carl F. H. Henry

_____
_____
_____
_____
_____
_____
_____
_____

What have you turned away from?

What is the one word you believe God would use to describe you?

What is a lie you no longer believe about yourself?

What thing(s) can you say "no" to now?

What friendship have you redefined?

A ship in harbor is safe, but that is not what ships are built for. William Shedd

RISE UP!

Who have you forgiven?

What soul ties did you sever?

Did you commit to pursue God and "crush the crush"
for a year?

What will you do to reach the world?

What are you going to do to stay awake?

The saddest thing is
a man who takes his
place on the stage of
life and forgets his
lines.

Winston Churchill

> You don't know what you're alive for until you know what you'd die for.
> Martin Luther King, Jr.

Oath of

I will remember what Jesus did for me an
that He deserves my all.

I will find my value in who God says I am
I'm worth His Son dying for me.

I will meditate on God's Word in areas I
have been weak in so that when I'm
tempted again, I will overcome. I refuse
to be a slave to sin any longer.

My best friends will be those that love
God with all of their hearts. Others
must be acquaintances. I will honor
my father and my mother.

I will guard my heart and focus on God
not a guy or a girl.

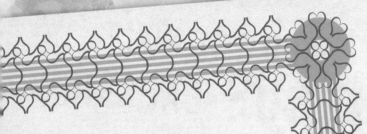

legiance

...will make my life count to reach this
...neration and the world!

...will be a disciple, always learning and
...ways growing.

_____

Enlisted Member Signature

_____

Date

BUILD ON YOUR
"RISE UP" EXPERIENCE

You've enlisted in the battle. You've finished Basic Training and you're ready to leave the bunker and venture *Over the Edge* into enemy lines. So where do you start?

Let *Over the Edge: Extreme Commitment* be your battle guide as you fight against Satan's lies. Over the next seven weeks, you will be challenged to live every day totally sold-out to Christ, your Master and Commander.

Now the battle begins! Working through *Over the Edge: Extreme Commitment* you'll learn to apply specific action steps that will help you become fully equipped to face the demands of the world and succeed as you live for Jesus.

HERE'S WHAT TO EXPECT:

>> Get a chance to dive deeper into the issues you looked at during *Rise Up: Basic Training for Warriors*
>> Be invited to dig into the Word every day
>> Discover specific strategies for countering the lies that have infiltrated your entertainment, your school, and all the places in between

Don't let one more day pass—learn to live a life of *Extreme Commitment!*

Order online at www.BattleCry.com
Call 1-800-323-7543
or visit your favorite local bookstore.